A HANDFUL OF VERSE

Songs and Other Poems

David Axtell

Published by Rough Tor Publishing
Torrs Park, Ilfracombe, Devon, EX34 8BA
www.ahstockwell.co.uk

First published in Great Britain, 2020

British Library Cataloguing-in-Publication Data.
A catalogue record for this book is available
from the British Library.

ISBN 978-1-5272-5881-5
Printed in Great Britain by
Arthur H. Stockwell Ltd
Torrs Park Ilfracombe
Devon EX34 8BA

Other Books by David Axtell

Birds for All Seasons

(An illustrated collection of poems)

(Published by Arthur H. Stockwell Ltd)

'David Axtell opens our eyes to birds, just being birds, and giving us endless enjoyment.' Rob Hume, ornithologist and author.

West of Windmill Hill

(Memories from a 1950s childhood in a Devon market town)

(Published by Arthur H. Stockwell Ltd)

'In his introduction the author declares he will be satisfied if he has managed to create something of the atmosphere of earlier times. In that he has succeeded.' *This England.*

Bude Haven – A History in Blank Verse

(Available at the Spencer Thorn bookshop, Bude)

Exeter – A Brief History in Blank Verse

Exeter – A Short Introduction in Verse

(Both held in the library of the Devon and Exeter Institution)

The Beast of Stoke Woods

(Published by Rough Tor Publishing)

(A crime mystery novel based in Exeter and the surrounding countryside)

'A very satisfying read.' Moya Eley, *Dartmoor News*.

'If you sit down at set of sun
And count the acts that you have done,
And, counting, find
One self-denying deed, one word
That eased the heart of him who heard,
One glance most kind
That fell like sunshine where it went –
Then you may count that day well spent.'

George Eliot

Contents

DEDICATION

To my wife, with thanks.

INVITATION

Reader, find a quiet place to look,
There turn the pages and at random view;
If nothing pleases, turn and look again –
A handful, or even less of them, will do.
If any then bring comfort or delight,
Relief from stress, give pleasure or ring true
A poet's task will not have been in vain
And what you've read will have been penned for you.

MEMORIES OF CHILDHOOD

Waking

As I lay half dreaming,
Before the sun was bright,
I heard a maiden singing
In the early morning light.

I heard a maiden singing,
When no one else was there,
In the valley far below
Where I'd dreamt I walked on air.

An echo filled the valley
Before the fading of the dream,
And I woke to see dust dancing
In the sunlight's golden beam.

I will not deceive her
And never let her go,
For I've heard a maiden singing
In the valley far below.

The Place

There is a place beside a stove
A mantelpiece above, on which a wireless stands,
Where, in the daytime, on the floor I play.
There at night my mother sings,
A door half open at the bottom of the stairs,
As in the dark I lie;
And when I wake, in early sun,
On half-remembered dreams to dwell,
Down to that place, in thought, again I go
And now the stove, the mantelpiece,
The wireless and a coloured jug I see
All bathed in golden light,
And I am filled with joyfulness
At greater joy to be.

Windmill Hill

When I sit upon the swing
I look across at Windmill Hill,
Forever green and always there,
Rising up towards the sky.
Back I push and grip the ropes
Then down I come and out I fly
Above the valley far below;
I bend my knees and swing back, high,
Drop and go right out once more.
In winter when I am indoors
And through the bedroom window stare,
In the sun or through the rain,
Windmill Hill I'll see again
Forever green and always there.

Day and Night

Above my head the sky is blue
    As I look up
    And all around,
High, as far as I can see
And coming right down to the ground,
As if I stand inside a bowl
Which just the sun shines through.

At night-time when the sky is free
    As I look up
    I see afar;
The sky above is full of light
While all around is near and dark
And as I close my eyes in sleep
The stars look down on me.

Summer Evening

The sun, all day so hot and bright,
Into the west is dropping low,
Shedding now a golden glow.
Through the gate I wheel the grass,
Across the yard and to the back.
Voices in the air ring clear,
Birds are hushed, as if they feel
The closeness of a state of bliss.
I see, before to bed I go
My mother smiling at the gate,
My father standing in the yard.
I shall, I know, remember this.
When, in my bed, I close my eyes,
I still see her at the gate,
Happy in her weariness
And hear their voices echoing
In the sunset's golden glow.

Looking Out

At a window, looking out,
Late afternoon, a rainy day,
Days growing short,
Nights closing in.
Down in the road, beyond the fence,
With headlights on and gentle hum,
The cars swish by and sideways spray.
People passing stare ahead
And do not look at me,
Nor see the room, where, in the stillness
And the flickering light,
Before the embers glow,
I stand and feel that here I've always been,
And shall forever be.

The Bathroom

In the lino, on the floor,
Dolphins, sharks and whales,
And sea creatures which have no name
And were never seen before.

Some there are which stare at me
With grinning eyes, and teeth,
Some are half-created forms
Emerging from the sea.

And yet they are not what they seem
Although they leer at me,
They do not come again at night
Like terrors in a dream.

Black creatures in a sea of green,
With grinning eyes, and teeth,
Some there are which have no name
Which I alone have seen.

In the Dark

When I am alone at night
And the corners of my room are dark,
And outside the trees are black
And the stairs begin to creak,
And shadows look like highwaymen
And start to fill my head with fears;
From the wall beside my bed
Come leering faces, from within,
And hands reach up from underneath;
My face grows hot and as I turn
I feel my pillow wet with tears,
Then I pray to safely sleep
And wake again in morning light.

The Snow

Earlier it had rained,
Then came the snow,
As I had hoped;
Slow, at first,
Then large flakes
Fell thick and fast
As I watched at the window,
Settling on the grass
To my delight.
Now road and hedge
And fields beyond,
Down the valley
Up the hill,
Turned white;
And the sky dropped down
And the clouds hung low
And all was silent,
As at night.

The Wind

In the coldest room I stand,
I'm inside, the wind's out there,
Outside the windows and the wall,
Up the drive and whistling round;
Invisible, it shakes the glass,
The macrocarpas bend and sway;
It seems to pause to catch its breath
Then comes and thuds against the house.
Silence falls, it starts to ease
Then disappears, I know not where.
Before it goes I hear it say
"I shall outlive you, one and all!"

SONGS OF SADNESS AND LOSS

Early Love

What happened to those happy hours,
The lately fallen dew,
The bursting buds of early spring,
None more fresh than you?

Where now are those timeless days,
Soft they flowed like streams?
The future then before us lay
Where too were all our dreams.

What, before our time is done,
Became of you and me?
Rivers swiftly onward run
And flow into the sea.

At a Railway Station

Whose are these faces,
Resembling only one?
Faces I seem to know
Which smile and pass
Without revealing their identity.

Whose are these forms,
Resembling only one?
Forms I seem to know,
They lean but quickly pass
Without revealing their identity.

Do all men dream and pay the price of dreams?
Faces and forms
Resembling one
Who loved and left
Without revealing her identity.

Remembering the Dead

Counting it a loss
To have discovered
    Let it lie;
In the earth the secret is hidden,
Let it not be uncovered.

Do not attempt it,
The life, from its death, is delivered,
    A broken bone
Is all the dead hero can show.

The dead preserve their silence,
In silence they are remembered.

Evening Chill

I feel the touch of autumn chill
  In evening air, too soon,
The sun but lately at its height
  Before the end of June.

Young apples sit upon the trees
  And weigh the branches down,
The winds have dried the chestnut leaves,
  With rust their tips are brown.

The sun will warm more summer days,
  Fruit ripen on the trees,
Among the flowers, in dappled light,
  Fly butterflies and bees.

Robin at Dawn

I wake from dreams to thought, to hear
A robin singing from a tree,
As summer fades, with thinning notes
Of things, I know, will never be

And all the things which never were;
The robin, sitting on the tree,
Unaware of who I am,
Is singing to another me.

Lament for the Older Ones

How much I liked the old ones, so much more
Than now, in general, I find I like the new,
I'd suffered less and had not seen a war
But they mostly listened, saw a point of view.
Words they used accompanied by thought,
Experience they had in plenty, were content,
At peace they were, held what they had been taught
And met with calm what life and heaven sent.
Where now are the tales of former years?
Where now the echoes of the minstrels' lays?
Where now the human laughter and the tears?
Where now the courtesy and pleasant ways
Before the skies were filled with tuneless drones
And ears made deaf to all but monotones?

Last Words

The words have been spoken, what I could I have done,
Sadness speaks loudest with a silent tongue,
Words melt like snow before the heat of the sun,
The words have been spoken, what I could I have done;
Like the streams from the glacier, let the tears run,
The lay of the minstrel is finally sung;
The words have been spoken, what I could I have done,
Sadness speaks loudest with a silent tongue.

LOVE SONGS AND SONNETS

Aubade

Calls a gentle dove
To my waking love –
Arise, put on your summer dress,
Come now! Come now!
Eyes will grow accustomed
To your loveliness.

Two Triolets – Youth and Age

1

Young lovers laugh away their fears
And dream of better days to be,
Before the passage of the years
Young lovers laugh away their fears;
Time may bring them pain and tears
And dreams become a memory,
Young lovers laugh away their fears
And dream of better days to be.

2

Dreams fall apart when we grow old
Unless, to love, we still aspire.
The old are cautious, youth is bold,
Dreams fall apart when we grow old;
Our lives are lived, our story's told
As passion cools, our hopes expire;
Dreams fall apart when we grow old
Unless, to love, we still aspire.

Two Sonnets

The Rose

Of all flowers most I love the rose,
In gardens, or wild with weeds and wayside trees,
Summer's heat its perfume will expose,
It dances in a gentle morning breeze;
On our cool shores it to full beauty grows,
So too in lands beyond far-distant seas;
Wherever, red or white, its blooms it shows
It's visited by butterflies and bees.
This much I've found in laughing lips and eyes,
In pleasing gestures and delightful ways,
There have I thought my true devotion lies,
On many faces let my tired eyes gaze.
But of all roses none I've found like this,
And on her lips discovered perfect bliss.

Constant Love

She, whom I love, to one is always true,
To one she gives, for one waits patiently –
When she's alone, no one waits like she;
To one she gave her heart when love was new,
Not for a day, or month, as others do,
Nor to one who was or soon might be
Deserving to receive such loyalty,
But as she does and as love would construe.
For when she loves, to hope she does aspire,
She sees love burning in a mist-veiled star;
Once love is lit it is a constant fire,
It is our best and who we really are.
In loving me she does not love in part,
Loves not at all unless with all her heart.

Love's Brevity

Love is swept into the past
If now is not eternity;
Lovers dream their love will last –
Love is swept into the past.
On flowing water dreams are cast
And life is but mortality;
Love is swept into the past
If now is not eternity.

BIRDS OF SEA AND SHORE

Turnstones

Daintily they prod and search
Among the rocks and weed
Beside the thundering sea;
Between the ocean and the land,
Where the tide turns,
At the water's edge
And the tongues of foam sweep
The untouched sand.
Mottled backs and orange legs,
They rise in flight and fall
On quick wings, as I approach,
With plaintive calls.
Not tame, but not completely wild,
They search the rocks and feed –
Untainted by humanity.

Sanderlings

With rapid runs they race across the strand,
Close to the torrent of the sea
They probe, for tiny forms of life, the sand.
They cross the freshly silvered shore,
Darting, on clockwork legs, with piping calls,
Forward they go with each receding wave,
Run back when each returns;
As I approach they rise on beating wings
With sudden noise, their wildness claim,
Till far from me, once more, they touch the land.

Gannets

On crowded rock face rising sheer,
The air with cries of thousands loud,
Fledglings sit, in coats of down;
Should they fall, it will be to death,
Ducked by skuas until they drown.

Out at sea, beyond the waves,
On a late returning tide,
Wings stretched wide, in solo flight,
A gannet skims the ocean face,
In the sunlight, shining white.

At sunset, out beyond the bay,
They gather, wheeling as they climb,
Till wings bent backward, falling free,
They drop like arrows, gaining speed,
And plummet deep into the sea.

BIRDS OF FIELD, MOOR AND RIVER

Lapwings

As I look up they catch my eye,
Flickering in uncertain flight,
I watch them as they cross the sky
On rounded wings, now black, now white,
Not many but at least a few,
To my delight.
They dip a little to the left
Then drop a little to the right,
Hesitant and delicate,
Not many but at least a few,
Before they vanish from my sight.

Skylark

Beating the air with all its might
It rises on the power of wings,
Up and up it soars in flight,
Beating the air with all its might
And soaring to still greater height
High above my head it sings,
Beating the air with all its might
It rises on the power of wings.

Barn Owl

With a single shriek it breaks the hush,
Unseen by me, in fading dusk;
Light on large wings
It strokes, with wafty sweeps, the air
And with another cry, not far away,
It haunts the vale.
As evening darkens into night
It listens for a rustling sound,
Then, talons drawn,
It drops, in silence, to the ground,
Deals sudden death
To mouse or vole – of which they're unaware.

The Owl at Night

The moon is full and clear the sky,
Beware, small creatures, of the owl!
Throughout the night, with searching eye,
A silent hunter's on the prowl.

Above the moors and wooded hills
A phantom haunts with muffled wing,
He hunts until he's had his fill
With eager stare and listening.

The sky is clear, the stars are bright,
Voles and mice keep very still!
While darkness lasts stay out of sight,
He'll hunt until he's had his fill.

The Buzzard

Gently gliding in the sky,
Large and languid,
Above the land it moves away,
In a spiral, round and round,
Inoffensive to creeping prey;
Up and up it soars until,
High in the troposphere,
Where insects teem
And swallows fly
And swifts, ecstatic, scream,
It becomes a speck;
Then disappears –
Invisible to human eye.

The Dipper

On moorland streams, where fast the flow,
It has its home, and does not stray,
Above clear water flying low,
Where bracken rusts and stones stain brown,
On searching fish and molluscs bent;
It lands where boulders stem the spate,
Long wide bib and round in chest,
Balanced, dips its little weight,
Then to the river drops and walks.
I saw one, dipping as it went,
Fishing in the stream alone,
Walking in the river, slow,
Beneath the water going down.
Generations here will stay,
Half hidden in the rowan's shade,
Fly up and down their moorland streams,
On finding little fish intent.

Red-legged Partridge

Across the lawn a red-legged partridge ran,
White chin framed in black,
Speckled breast, red bill and eye;
From behind a bush I saw it peer,
Then, like a sprinter, cross the open space
When other birds would fly.
Glad was I, to see it
Through the middle of the garden run,
Legs straight and head held high,
Fearless of any predator or gun.

Heron Flying Homeward

The heron, like an oarsman, plies
In gentle and unhurried flight,
Large and slowly flapping wings;
Homeward flies in fading light.

Homeward flies in fading light
To its place beneath the tree;
With large and slowly flapping wings,
As the sun goes down beneath the sea.

BLACKBIRDS SINGING

1

On the chimney, early spring,
The blackbird brightly sings,
Sings to claim its new estate,
Sings to keep its new-found mate.

The garden's bare, the gulls have fled,
Finches and buntings fed,
In the fading of the light
It fills the empty space of night.

Thinly clad in folded wings,
Still the blackbird sings,
Under a cold and darkening sky
It sings its song, not asking why.

2

I love to hear the blackbird sing
When dew is fresh, at break of day,
In the early days of spring,
Before the scented buds of may.
Before the baking of the hay.

I love to hear the blackbird's song
When the sun is in the sky,
When the balmy days are long,
When the willows gently sigh,
When the clouds are small and high.

But most I love to hear it sing
In the evening after rain,
When the hay is gathered in,
When the barn is full of grain,
Then I hear it sing again.

FLOWERS, BUTTERFLIES AND BEES

Sonnet

In a world where billions are but one
I sit where flowers, weeds and grasses are,
Butterflies, flickering, come or do not come,
Float on the wind or drop to test their power.
Drawn by the scent or colour of the flower
As butterflies in time have always done,
The pollen and sweet nectar they devour
Or go, without despair, when there is none.
In time unknown to us they come and go,
As long before we gave them names or thought
Of worlds, or time, or butterflies or aught,
Wherever flowers, weeds and grasses grow,
In random flight, unconscious and unsought,
In a world in which we live but do not know.

The Roses

See the roses, yours and mine,
Red and yellow intertwine,
The roses, the roses,
Red and pink and yellow.

See the roses, yours and mine,
Who will mar them with a sign?
The roses, the roses,
Who will dare to touch them?

Learning Butterflies

Fluttering upward in the light,
On delicate and coloured wings,
From places hidden from our sight –
Chrysalis and winter sleep,
Appearing when the sun is bright.

Clouded yellow, orange tip
To meadow, moor and hedge,
Brimstone, comma, common blue,
Small heath, marsh fritillary,
Gatekeeper, grayling too.

Flying from across the sea
In clouds to countryside and town,
They land on flowers, roadside trees,
In the sunshine spread their wings
On walls or on our hats or knees.

Painted lady, swallowtail,
On thistle, flower and sedge,
Small tortoiseshell and cabbage white,
Monarch and red admiral,
All fluttering in the light.

Among the flowers a dancing pair
With lacewings, dragonflies and bees;
Circling and rising in the air,
Above the chimney pot they go
Out of sight, we don't know where.

Skipper, ringlet, speckled wood,
From scrub to mountain edge,
Copper, hairstreak, meadow brown,
Peacock, purple emperor,
Fluttering up and down.

Red Admiral

It spreads its wings before my eyes,
Black, ember-red and white as snow,
Deepening in the evening sun,
On the wing-tips tiny dots,
Captured fires of sunlight glow.

The Bees

Lost in a meadow with no trees
But tall grass topped with seeds,
And flowers, yellow, white and blue,
Scabious, clover, feverfew,
Uphill a hedge, the sky beyond;
Here I lie, no higher than the weeds,
I am with the pollen-bearing bees.

DEATH OF A RAVEN

A Ballad

A raven from its craggy haunt,
Just at break of day,
Flew out above the whispering sea
And went in search of prey.

Fledglings stirred inside the nest
Beneath a mother's eye;
Go out and search for flesh and blood
Or stay and watch them die.

The raven soared above the cliff
Then swung towards the town,
Above the houses seagulls wheeled
And jackdaws stood around.

Down to a chimney stack it swooped
And muted fledgling calls;
Go out and search for flesh and blood,
It flapped and spread its claws.

A jackdaw raised the hue and cry,
To the rooftop flew a pair,
Gulls and jackdaws circled round
With clamour filled the air.

With empty beak the raven leapt
And rose on beating wings,
With furious eye turned right and left
But could not break the ring.

Less furious and more in fear
Still back and forth it flew,
They harried from above, below,
At length it wearier grew.

To the ground it dropped at last,
With crumpled wings it lay,
A sparrowhawk from within the hedge
Flew out to claim its prey.

The raven rose to face its foe
Or knew that it would die,
Long they battled, beak and claw
Its wings too weak to fly.

With wailing cries two cats appeared
The sparrowhawk flew away,
The raven had no strength to move
And in the shadows lay.

Fledglings stirred inside a nest
Beneath a mother's eye,
A bird went out in search of flesh
Or knew that they would die.

SONGS OF CORNISH PLACES

A View of Week St Mary

Beside a five-barred gate I stand
  Beneath a naked tree,
Silent at the snow's command
  A world of white I see.

Whitened fields before me lie,
  With hints of mirrored blue,
The landscape spreads towards a sky
  Of pale and roseate hue.

A church tower sits upon a hill
  With bells immobile hung,
Time's in abeyance, of Sundays still
  A month since they have rung.

At sheep I stare and static lambs
  Across the frozen lea,
The lambs are running to their dam,
  The sheep stare back at me.

Beside a wall I stand and see
  A picture in a frame
Recall from anonymity
  A presence and a name.

Widemouth Bay

Where the tide runs swift and sweeps the foam
Across the silver saturated sand,
Where waves turn and backward toss their spray,
Or crash on rocks, thud in canyons
Or thump upon the solid land;

Where water runs in gurgling streams
Between the rocks and into pools and whirls,
Where gobies shoot like bullets into holes,
Purple flowers finger gently
And green-hair seaweed furls, unfurls

And runnels swing the buoyant bladderwrack,
Where I hear the thunder of the sea,
And listen to the seething ripples sing,
There have I stood alone since time
Grown old and there I love to be.

Crackington Haven

Today we went to Crackington Haven
  And walked the narrow beach,
From grassy cliffs, which soar each side,
  We watched the gannets fly and dive
Before the turning of the tide.
  Today we went to Crackington Haven,
  Tomorrow we may see a raven.

Today we went to Crackington Haven
  And tasted the salt of the sea,
We followed the stream and crossed the bridge,
  Climbed again to the top of the cliff
To watch the gulls from the edge of the ridge.
  Today we went to Crackington Haven,
  Tomorrow we may see a raven.

Above a Cove on the Lizard Peninsula

They tip and tilt and rock and sway,
Within the harbour, in the bay,
Fast along the high stone wall,
Side by side they rise and fall,
From morning tide, to eventide.
At night, set loose, they wander out
Beyond the rocks, beneath the stars
And now the ocean's waves they ride.

Land's End

But I was called away,
In the heat of the open day,
From the ocean's heave
To take my leave,
Home to my haven of hope.

Sadly, I lingered there,
On the cliffs where rocks are bare,
And seagulls swing
With extended wing
Down to the sun-shone sea.

And I made, to myself, a vow
To remember this moment, now,
When to one, simple-hearted,
A truth was imparted,
Thus home to my haven of hope.

Leaving Cornwall

Away from the wash of the shore,
And the ring of the floating bell,
The wind o'er the wild moor
Where the ponies dwell.

Away from the grassy cliff,
Where the lark goes soaring high,
The mists of the sea drift,
And the salt winds fly.

MOMENTS AND MOODS

The Plane

Shining silver with vapour trail
It heads up high into clear blue sky,
And I'm in the past, with the eyes of a child,
The moon, a half-wafer, sits nearby.

No vapour now, then comes the sound,
And I'm no more the child on the summer's day,
But still the sky's blue, noises are few,
As the drone of the engine dies away.

A Blackbird's Look

I stopped on the step
And it paused as it flew to a tree
With a cry of alarm;
It chirped, as it stared,
To the bird in the nest
Which was hidden from sight to me.

It flew to the hedge
As I entered the house, but before,
I thought once again
Of its pause on the tree
And the look it returned –
Could they have been something more?

A Blackbird at Dusk

As dusk darkens to gloom,
A blackbird sings from a tree,
  Not for his space,
  Nor to his mate,
But his song is not unheard
By one who sits in an unlit room,
But he does not sing to me.

I sit alone in a room,
He sings but not to me,
  As a bird a million
  Years ago
Sang and was not unheard
By one who listened, alone in the gloom,
As he sat beneath a tree.

On a Summer Evening

Clouds were rising in the north,
The sun was dropping low,
I'd still a job to do outside
And, having left it, had to go.

As out I stepped, down came the rain,
It ran from roof to spout,
Down the garden paths it poured,
To roadside gutters flowing out.

Soon the road became a stream,
And, running down the hill,
The flooding water higher rose
Until the cars were still.

The sun was setting in the west,
Roofs and lamp posts gleamed,
It was as if on works of men
A glorious light had beamed.

I was not looking for a sign
Nor did the moment last,
But a swift came down from clouds above
And, swooping, through a rainbow passed.

Walk before Sunset in Spain

Today I let others sweat and bronze on the beach,
A goldfinch tunes my ear to the gentle song
Of the wild oats, sowing already their seeds among
Fields of poppy and corn marigold. To reach
Tall cliffs and my dreams I leave behind the throng,
My feet still sore from the stinging rocks of Calella.
Pine for my nostrils, soon my tongue, I long
For the soft winds and juniper of Agua Gellida.
I cool my feet on the shingle of Tamariu
Then climb towards Mont Esperant's vines and mist;
When the setting sun stains red the Pyrenees
And bindweed folds its petals in the dew,
Goat bells summon me to vespers, or a tryst,
Where a hoopoe waits alone beneath the trees.

Solitude

Along a lane not built for cars, but carts,
Where hedges are not hewn but left to grow
And birds, still wild, unsighted, come and go,
Alone I wander, not now in fits and starts;
Above, the sky is clear and free of sound,
No sound intrudes to draw me back to time,
Flowers in blossom, blackberries abound,
On hazel branches, stems of bryony climb.
To solitude are we born and who we are,
Passing from darkness to the light of day;
In time I'll look again to find my way
Beyond this hill to distances afar,
But now, as long as human noises cease,
Here shall I be, contented and at peace.

Christmas Eve

Snow lies thick upon the frozen earth,
Peace returns to heart of man and beast,
A silent world awaits a holy birth.
The sky, with stars, is full of silver light,
Joy is in the world on Christmas night.

Peace returns to heart of man and beast,
With bated breath and hope and fear reborn,
Each awaits in prayer the ancient feast.
The sky, with stars, is full of silver light,
Joy is in the world on Christmas night.

FIVE LATIN POEMS – TRANSLATIONS

Carpe Diem (Horace)

Do not ask, it's not for us to know our destiny,
Leuconoe, nor dabble in Babylonian numbers.
Whatever's to be, accept it, as we must –
Whether that's many more winters, or our last
Now beats the Tyrrhenian Sea against the rocks.
Pour out the wine, as envious time speeds past.
Seize the day, in tomorrow put no trust.

Vixi Puellis *(Horace)*

Until lately, in love's wars
I've done okay;
Time now to lay down my weapons,
No more pluck the strings;
Though you'd have to say
When it comes to girls
I've chalked up scores!

Now, on the left wall,
Let them remain
In the temple of Venus, born in foam –
Crowbar, torch and bow;
I've done with the pain,
In games of chance
I've made my calls.

O divine goddess of the sea
Of Cyprus and the heat
Of Memphis, far from Sithonian snows,
Raise a whip to arrogant Chloe –
Above her seat,
And let her have it,
Once, from me!

Pyrrha (Horace)

What slender youth, damp with perfume,
Among the roses in your cave
Presses himself upon you, Pyrrha,
And to your artless tresses is a slave?

Alas, too soon, all will be changed,
How often he'll be shedding tears,
Rough seas will catch him unawares
And bring him misery beyond his years.

Sad men, who gaze upon your golden hair,
Trust that loving you will always be;
My sodden clothes hang on the wall –
An offering to the god who rules the sea.

You Ask, Lesbia (Catullus)

You ask, Lesbia, how many of your kisses
Satisfy, or more than slake Catullus' thirst.
As many as the grains of sand of Libya,
In Cyrene, where silphium, between dry-mouthed
Jove's oracle and old Battus' sacred tomb
Grows, or as many as the stars on silent nights
Which look down and spy the secret lovers' tryst:
Enough or less – beyond what prying minds can tell –
Will do for those by mad Catullus kissed
And on which no evil tongue can cast a spell.

Vitam Beatiorem (Martial)

Life can be happier, I shall tell you why,
My dear Martial; the things which make this so are these:
Not money made through work, but inherited wealth;
A good farm, a fire in the hearth which all year burns;
No lawsuits, a toga rarely worn, a mind
At peace; strength of a man free-born, bodily health;
A sensible openness, compatible friends;
Easy company, a table of simple fare;
No drunken nights, but those which are worry-free;
Pleasure in bed, but no infidelity;
Sleep which brings darkness quickly to an end;
Being happy with oneself, not wanting more;
No fear of, nor longing for, the day you die.